The Top 20 Illustrated Asian and American Destinations [with Pictures]:

3 Books in 1

BY

The lost Traveler.

Disclaimer and Terms of Use:

Effort has been made to ensure that the information in this book is accurate and complete, however, the author and the publisher do not warrant the accuracy of the information, text and graphics contained within the book due to the rapidly changing nature of science, research, known and unknown facts and internet.

The Author and the publisher do not hold any responsibility for errors, omissions or contrary interpretation of the subject matter herein. This book is presented solely for motivational and informational purposes only.

THE LOST TRAVELER

"Traveler for 365 Days"

The Lost
TRAVELER

For over 80 years, "The Lost Traveler" has been a trusted resource offering expert travel advice for every stage of a traveler's journey. We hire local writers who know their destinations better than anyone, allowing us to provide the best travel advice for all tastes and budgets in over 7,500 destinations around the world. Our books make it possible for every trip to be the trip of a lifetime.

Our mission is to make every country accessible for any type of wallet and family.

Our key phrase is: *"If you haven't toured the world at least once, it's as if you've never really known the place where humanity has always lived"*

TABLE OF CONTENT

The Top 9+1 Asian Destinations for family and Co.

The Top 9+1 North America Destinations
for family and Co

The Top 9+1 South America Destinations for family and Co.

The Top 9+1 Asian Destinations for family and Co.

Everything you need to know to travel Asia on a Budget with your family and make your dream holiday become reality in 2021.

BY

The lost Traveler.

TABLE OF CONTENT

Top Asian places to visit

INTRODUCTION:

Lust and wonder to visit new exotic and beautiful places is everyone's passion and will. No wonder why such new and exciting experience help you gain great and wonderful memories. Right now I would mention some of the top beautiful and magnificent places that would catch your attention and captivate you towards the beauty around us. Some of them I would discuss would be different countries with wonderful sites, including Turkey, Pakistan, India, Singapore, Nepal, Philippine, China, Japan, Indonesia, Malaysia, and Thailand. Let's see how magnificent and beautiful places are there with different food dishes and culture. Such places are the best spot for family to visit and enjoy with a small amount of cash.

1. TURKEY

Turkey is one of those countries with most fascinating and lots of beautiful places with fancy dishes. It has many sites and is very cheap to visit and enjoy such in a small amount of money. There many cities full of outstanding and iconic places such as:

1. Antalya

Antalya is a beautiful city with an abundance of things for you to see and do also it is the fifth-most crowded city in Turkey and the capital of Antalya Province. Situated on Anatolia's southwest coast lined by the Taurus Mountains, Antalya is the biggest Turkish city on the Mediterranean coast outside the Aegean district with more than 1,000,000 individuals in its metropolitan region.

- **Lara Beach**

Lara Beach is a flawless spot to just kick back and unwind while taking in some rays. With the Mediterranean Sea full of beautiful sites and lapping at the shore as you enjoy in the sun, it is a serene spot with bunches of traveler workplaces, so you can undoubtedly get a drink or plunk down for a feast at one of the close-by eateries.

- **Hotels**

  Also in Lara beach there are five stars hotel to accommodate you and have a pleasant visit in small amount of money, such iconic titanic hotel with great view and sceneries.

- **Kursunlu Waterfalls**
- Kursunlu is a waterfall set in the midst of a cool, pine woods. Strolling at Kursunlu Nature Park, in the midst of the extraordinary environment scented with blackberries, wild roses, and the smells of numerous different plants, may prompt an opportunity of experiencing with bunnies, squirrels, woodpeckers, turtles or other little creatures. With millions of people around the world would come.

2. Istanbul

Istanbul is a significant city in Turkey that rides Europe and Asia across the Bosporus Strait. Its Old City reflects social impacts of the numerous empires that once controlled and ruled here. Also it is one of the most iconic cities for tourists and foreigners which has attracted millions of people attraction with its historic and most influential places. Like Hagia Mosque, Blue Mosque and many other places for family to visit and enjoy.

- **Hagia Mosque:**
- Hagia Sophia can be considered the best and most visited sights in Istanbul, and the adjoining Topkapi Palace. Hagia Sophia is a previous church and gallery and pronounced as one of the world's most prominent historical works and acknowledged as the world's eighth miracle. And it is the Muslim mosque now.

Topkapı Palace

Topkapı Palace is the subject of more vivid stories than many of the world's exhibition halls set up. Licentious kings, aggressive squires, excellent courtesans, and conspiring eunuchs lived and worked here between the fifteenth and nineteenth hundreds of years when it was the court of the Ottoman realm. A visit to the royal residence's rich structures, a gem filled Treasury, and rambling Harem gives a captivating look into their lives. Best place to visit in the country and also a great historic and iconic site for tourists.

2.Ephesus

Europe's most finished traditional city, Ephesus is an antiquated site situated in Aegean Turkey. By the first century BC, Ephesus was perhaps the biggest city on the whole of the Roman Empire, bragging one the Seven Wonders of the Ancient World, the Temple of Artemis. The vestiges of Ephesus are all around saved and contained inside an enormous archeological site, making it one of Turkey's most mainstream vacation destinations.

Ephesus was proclaimed a Roman settlement in 133 BC, in spite of the fact that it didn't arrive at its top until around 200 years after the fact. At a certain point, when the city was the capital of Roman Asia Minor, Ephesus housed in excess of 250,000 perpetual occupants. St.Paul lived in Ephesus, encouraging Christianity among numerous different religions. With the decrease of the harbor of Ephesus and the terminating of the city by Germanic Goths in the third century, Ephesus started its decay.

2. PAKISTAN

Pakistan is the under developing country with so much potential and has most beautiful places and tourists points for people to visit. It is the 2nd biggest Muslim country. With so many natural beauty and wonderful sites such as:

1.Islamabad

The city is known for the remarkable and astonishing number of parks and forests, including the Margalla Hills National Park and the Shakarparian. The city is the 2nd beautiful capital in the world and home to a few milestones, with the most outstanding one being the Faisal Mosque – the biggest mosque in South Asia and the fifth-biggest planet. Best place to visit and it has places like:

2.Faisal Mosque

The Faisal Mosque is a mosque in Islamabad, Pakistan. Upon completion it was the largest mosque in the world; it is currently the fifth largest mosque in the world and the largest in South Asia. It is located on the foothills of Margalla Hills in Islamabad.

- **Shakarparian National Park**
- Shakarparian is a hill and a national and amusement park located near the Zero Point Interchange in Islamabad, Pakistan. Pakistan Monument and Pakistan Monument Museum are also located in Shakarparian.

3. Kashmir

4. Kashmir is one the most beautiful and eye catching destination in Pakistan, it has most breathtaking and loving scenes. It is regarded as heaven on earth in Pakistan, because of its natural beauty and pleasant places such as Neelum valley,Banjosa lake, and Toli Pir.

- **Neelum Valley**
- Kashmir's most beautiful valley is Neelum Valley, the scenes here most captivating and heart touching, people are most hospitable and generous.

- **Toli pir**
- Toli pir is a most magnificent hilltop in Kashmir and known as popular and eye catching place for whole people around the world.

4, Swat

Swat is a district in Pakistan and is most famous for its mountains and lakes and it is considered family and tourist spot. Smack valley is a delightful valley in the Northern Part of Pakistan. It is very much associated with Islamabad the Capital City of Pakistan through the Road. Subsequent to entering in the Swat Valley you can see the Snow Clad Mountain structure the significant distance. It is an absolute necessity to visit the valley in Pakistan. Like

- **Kalam**
- kalam is situated in swat and is popular for its forest, lakes and mountains.

- **Mingora**
- Mingora is a city in swat district; it is the 3rd biggest in swat as it is filled with mountains and hilltops for its visitors. Best place for family and friends to visit.

- **Mahodand Lake**
- Known for its freezing water and wealth of trout fish, the lake is situated in the Ushu Matiltan valley around 40 kilometers above Kalam. Mahodand Lake is a lake situated in the upper Usho Valley a ways off of around 35 kilometers from Kalam in Swat District of Khyber Pakhtunkhwa region of Pakistan.

1. CHINA

China is one of the biggest countries in the world not only populated but it is teemed with most exotic places as well let's take look at these for families and friends to visit. And also it is full with so many historical and cultural places.

1. **Huairo**

2. It is a district in china with one of the wonders around the world such as Great Wall of China.

- **Great wall of china**
- The Great Wall of China is a progression of fortresses that were worked across the borders northern lines of old Chinese states and Imperial China as assurance of safety against different roaming groups from the Eurasian Steppe.

2.Beijing

Beijing, China's rambling capital, has history extending back 3 centuries. However it's referred to as much for present day architecture as its old destinations, for example, the stupendous Forbidden City intricate, the magnificent royal residence during the Ming and Qing lines.

- **The Forbidden City and the Imperial Palace**
- The Palace Museum is a public historical center housed in the Forbidden City at the center of Beijing. It was set up in 1925 after the last Emperor of China was ousted from his castle and made its way for people in general.

2.Sichuan

Sichuan is a great province in a china which is known for outstanding and marvelous architecture such as Leshan Giant Bhudda.

- **Leshan Giant Bhudda**
- Various little Buddhas were cut around this immense sculpture. Individuals even unearthed the bluff burial places of the Han Dynasty around the Leshan Giant Buddha. Different noteworthy locales make the Leshan Giant Buddha especially significant for archeologists and exploring individuals' ways of life in old occasions.

This stone sculpture cut during the Tang Dynasty stands 71 meters high at the meeting purpose of the Minjiang, Dadu, and Qingyi streams. Explorers can see the Leshan Buddha during a waterway visit, where boats drift down the creek and pass the figure, or during a climbing endeavor, where gatherings give along with the bluff's highest point just as scale the feet of the Buddha. The Leshan is the most significant stone Buddha design on the planet and has been recorded as a UNESCO world legacy site since 1996; don't miss it!

2. India

India is the second most populous country in the world with great amazing places to visit and spent your time there, while this country is full of great heritage and perfect places in the world. Hospitality and love is part of their tradition and multiple religions are common here.

1.Amritsar

Amritsar is the biggest and most significant city in Punjab and is a significant business, social, and transportation focus. Likewise, it is the focal point of Sikhism and the site of the Sikhs' chief spot of love—the Harmandir Sahib, or Golden Temple.

Historical otherwise called Rāmdāspur and conversationally as Ambarsar, is the second most crowded city in the Indian territory of Punjab. The city is the authoritative base camp of the Amritsar region and is situated in the Majha area of Punjab.

• Ladakh

Ladakh is generally acclaimed for stunning scenes, the clear skies, the most elevated mountain passes, exciting experience exercises, Buddhist Monasteries, and celebrations.

- **Goa Beach**

- Goa is likewise known for its sea shores, and is most loveable place to enjoy with your family and friends. Most popular places known for beaches is only Goa Beach.

- **The Dudhsagar Waterfalls**
- The Dudhsagar Waterfalls are arranged on the Goa-Karnataka line and are one of India's must-see sights. The four-layered cascade structure is one of the tallest in India and is situated on the Mandovi River. The white waterfalls from a tallness of almost 1017 feet off a nearly steep mountain face. They structure a piece of the Bhagwan Mahaveer Sanctuary and Mollem National Park, so the ideal approach to contact them is by entering the public park and taking a van distributed by the recreation center to the falls.

The Dudhsagar journey inside the recreation center is shut to general society; however, you can arrive at the cascades by traveling from Kulem and following the jeep trail. Another conceivable course is the trip from Castle Rock in Karnataka. Coming at the waterfalls won't be a simple errand; however, it merits each ounce of exertion put into it. They are best capable during the storms as they lose their power during the dry season.

- **Agra**

Agra is quite possibly the most-visited urban community in India when the Mughal Empire's capital, Agra, is presently home to the impressive design known as the Taj Mahal.

- **Taj Mahal**
- While spectacularly delightful, the Taj Majal can be extremely packed. Likewise worth finding in Agra is the Agra Fort, which is very much like the Red Fort of Delhi. You can visit this sixteenth century fortress and even investigate the inside of its wonderful royal residence.

3. Nepal

Nepal, a landlocked country among India and China, is known for its mountain tops. The little nation contains eight of the ten most elevated tops on the planet, including Mount Everest and Kanchenjunga – the world's tallest and third tallest separately.

1.Khumbu Valley

Celebrated for its breathtaking mountain tops and the devotion and hospitality of its residents (the Sherpas), the Everest district (Khumbu) is quite possibly the most mainstream objections for vacationers in Nepal.

- **Gokyo Valley**
- Perhaps the most beautiful valleys in Nepal, the Gokyo valley, lies towards the west of the more popular Khumbu locale of the Himalaya. The peaceful valley flaunts broad fields for yaks to munch during summer, and the flawless turquoise lakes are just amazing. Gokyo can be visited after journeying up to Everest Base Camp by adding five days to the schedule.

On the off chance that Gokyo is your principal objective, at that point, the journey goes up the Everest trail just to the extent the teahouses at Kenjoma (where the path from Khumjung joins the absolute path). The way leads up towards Mong La pass before dropping steeply down to the Dudh Koshi River banks. The trail at that point goes past rhododendron and oak timberlands and cascades, which are regularly frozen. Two or three hours on this captivating path, and you show up in Dole, whereyou go through the night in a teahouse.

1.Kathmandu

Kathmandu is especially renowned for its religious landmarks. Different sanctuaries, temples, cloisters, monasteries, and stupas embellish the city's scene, especially the Pashupatinath Temple and the Changu Narayan, which are well known for their shocking, complex strict works of art.

- **Pashupatinath temple**
- Pashupatinath temple is a sacred and most significant religious destinations in Asia for lovers of Shiva. Inherent in the fifth century and later redesigned by Malla rulers, the actual site is said to have a unique history and existed from the earliest starting point of the thousand years when a Shiva lingam was found.

3. Bhaktapur

Bhaktapur has the best-safeguarded castle yards and old downtown area in Nepal and is recorded as a World Heritage Site by UNESCO for its rich culture, sanctuaries, wood, metal, and stone works of art. It stays the best safeguarded of the three, regardless of the harm of the 2015 earthquake. It stays the best saved of the three, in spite of the harm of the 2015 tremor.

- **Nyatapola Temple**

Nyatapola Temple is an eighteenth century sanctuary situated in Bhaktapur, Nepal. It is the tallest structure in the valley and the tallest sanctuary in the country. The sanctuary was implicit 1702 and is devoted to Goddess Siddhi Lakshmi, a manifestation of Goddess Parvati. The icon of the Goddess, which is introduced in the sanctum sanctorum, is accepted to be incredibly fearsome. Albeit just the sanctuary ministers enter the sanctum sanctorum, guests can investigate the remainder of the sanctuary. The landmark has endure two significant seismic tremors in the area and has endured minor harms. It is additionally, hence, known for its underlying strength.

4. Singapore

Being overly perfect, Singapore as a perfect city, it is famous for having probably the cleanest roads on the planet, generally because of a 50,000-in number cleaning labor force utilized to keep the streets clean.

1.Gardens by the bay

Gardens by the Bay are a tremendous, bright, advanced park in the territory of Singapore. Among the highlights are the acclaimed Super tree structures. These offer a great skywalk over the garden, with curiously large shell formed nurseries that reproduce Perfect Mountain like shapes, which are quite attractive for the tourists.

A hint of God's creation is found only contiguous the Marina Reservoir. This park with 101 hectares of the land zone is a recovered land in focal Singapore. This is Gardens by the Bay, a grand desert spring abounding with displays and pleasures. You can discover relaxation and sporting exercises, instructive projects, and visits to these nurseries. Also, a visit here allows you to connect with nature.

There are many attractions in the Gardens by the Bay; all you require is to pick which one will suit your taste. This is likewise extraordinary for family holding, the date for two, and an association among your circles.

1. Singapore flyer

2. Considered as the world's most giant perception wheel, the Singapore Flyer took over two years to assemble following its essential function in September 2005. It stands 165-meter-tall and is one of the best tourist spots, especially for family and friends, but it is also the most beautiful piece of work.

Singapore Flyer is a goliath Ferris Wheel. In the event that statures thrill you, at that point this is a ride that you would thoroughly appreciate. It is one of the tallest Ferris wheels on the planet today.

The perspectives from high up are amazing, and one can get a brief look at Singapore in a solitary go. Appreciate this exciting experience on your excursion to Singapore, and after the ride investigate some close by places in Singapore as well. Peruse on, to understand what everything is accessible close by to do in Singapore.

2. Pulau Ubin

While Pulau Ubin is a historical and ancient place where some granite stones are accepted to be over 200 years of age, granite quarries gave the underlying attraction to early neighborhood settlement, and a significant part of the granite was utilized for Singapore's initial turns of events. A heaven for nature sweethearts, Pulau Ubin, has a lot to bring to the table with its rich greenery and bountiful untamed life. Visit the unwanted quarries and become familiar with their local plants as you wander around the island.

- **Chek jawa**

The Chek Jawa wetlands are one of the fundamental attractions of Pulau Ubin and home to a flourishing biological ecological system of the country's biggest assortment of natural life. To get to Chek Jawa, you need to stop your bike and walk since the footpaths are delicate and tight. The wetlands generally comprise of mangroves, rough shores and a sandy shore. During low tide, hope to see the little marine animals like mudskippers, crabs and more modest fish. For a more extravagant comprehension of the natural life in Check Jawa, join a guided strolling visit and gain from the specialists.

5. Philippines

The Philippines is a modest travel destination, even by Southeast Asian principles. A few inns might be more costly than you would expect; however, all in all, it is a truly moderate travel objective.

1.Ifugao

Ifugao, a place for wet-rice agriculturalists possessing northern Luzon's hilly territory, Philippines has made the places with beautiful outlooks. Their incredible arrangement of watered rice porches steeply formed, mountain-terraced dividers of stone that lean marginally internal at the top is widely acclaimed and was created with an essential innovation.

- **Banaue**
- Banaue, the arrangement of flooded rice porches in the mountains of north-focal Luzon, Philippines, made over 2,000 years prior by the Ifugao public, now it is the most beautiful and exotic place for the

family to visit. Also situated in a few towns, they are aggregately known as the Banaue rice.

1. **Palawan**

2. Palawan Island Philippines is renowned for white beaches, clear water and astonishing biodiversity, additionally for Puerto Princesa Underground River. Palawan is the first run through on the platform. Best place for families to visit and enjoy.

- **Coron Island**
- Coron is a tropical island in the territory of Palawan in the Philippines. Coron is most famous for a-list World War II-time wreck. The island likewise offers limestone karst scenes, lovely beaches, perfectly clear freshwater lakes, and shallow-water coral reefs.

- **Puerto Princesa**

This underground waterway framework's feature is that it streams straightforwardly into the ocean, with its saline lower half exposed to flowing impact. The waterway's sinkhole presents striking, eye-catching rock arrangements.

2.Mountain province

Mountain province is one of the most fascinating and beautiful province in Philipines and it is known for its beautiful and wonderful places for tourist to visit.

- **Sagada**
- Sagada is known for its grand mountain valleys, rice fields, reviving waterfall, limestone caverns, and ocean of mists.

6. Japan

Japan is known worldwide for its customs, arts, including tea functions, calligraphy, and many other festivals. The nation has a tradition of special nurseries, gardens, figure, and verse. Japan is home to more than multiple UNESCO World Heritage locales and is the origin of sushi, generally well known.

1. **Naoshima**

2. Well surrounded adequately by the Seto Inland Sea's shimmering waters, the unspoiled island of Naoshima lies between the beautiful Japanese islands of Honshu and Shikoku. Its dazzling view, extraordinary contemporary craftsmanship, historical centers, and various outside models are an exceptionally famous traveler and tourist spot and destination.

Naoshima Island, otherwise called Japan's Art Island, is acclaimed for its craft galleries and outside models.

Most popular is the "giant pumpkin" by craftsman Yayoi Kusama, the informal symbol for Naoshima. As far as I might be concerned, visiting Naoshima got going as an insane pumpkin chasing mission; however, it transformed into an out-and-out relationship. To help other people visiting, I've assembled a guide of activities in Naoshima.

3. Shirakawa-go & Gokayama

4. Celebrated for their breathtaking settings and traditionally covered rooftop farmhouses, they consider as a real part of focal Honshu's most famous vacation spots.

While this implies they can become very busy, especially during Golden Week and the cherry bloom season, the towns genuinely are a treat to visit. This is because the unmistakable gassho-zukuri structures that look so dazzling encompassed by prolific farmland and eminent nature loan them an enchanting, serene, and provincial feel.

Shirakawa-go is a famous for its familiar scene and covered rooftop homes. This article presents must-see spots, nearby dishes and road food, and headings to this touring objective.

5. Nikko

6. Nikko is situated in the northwestern of Tochigi Prefecture, most famous for its vast and rich nature, just as the numerous celebrated touring spots, including original altars and sanctuaries. As it used to be the hallowed place and sacred where there is mountain love, innumerable individuals visit the site for its unmistakable otherworldly climate.

The Shinkyo connect resembles the access to Nikko's sanctuaries and sanctums mind-boggling, the ideal spot to begin your excursion from. The actual scaffold is important for the Futarasan Shrine, one of the trees in Nikko that love Mount Futara as a "shintai". In the Shinto religion, a shintai is an item wherein a heavenly nature can live, giving an actual structure available to its devotees.

A legend says that when Saint Shodo showed up here, the water straeam was so solid he was unable to cross the waterway. A divine being encouraged him by sending two snakes that transformed into an extension.

4.Tokyo

Tokyo's cultural side is well known for its various activities and top attractions, including historical centers, celebrations, universally noted cooking, and elite athletics clubs, including baseball, football, and customary Japanese pursuits like sumo wrestling.

Tokyo, opposite the Ariake Coliseum, one of the scenes for the impending Tokyo 2020 Olympic Games, involves 8,000 square meters of a four-story expanding on the edges of the city. The amusement park comprises of six regions dependent on various topics, with entire areas committed to Sailor Moon and Evangelion. The scenes are a mashup of the real world and fiction: Space Center presentation portrays the dispatch of a Saturn V space transport from the 1970s, while the Global Village includes shockingly precise entertainments of five urban communities in Asia and Europe with fantastical augmentations like mythical serpents and robots tossed in for no particular reason.

7. Indonesia

Indonesia is among the region known for the fire region, an area with probably the most dynamic volcanoes on the planet. A significant number of the nation's volcanoes, for example, Mount Merapi, are famous for their vicious emissions, and they're shocking, however most popular one now.

Mount Bromo

Mount Bromo is likely quite possibly the most renowned grand attraction in East Java of Indonesia. It is well known for its superb dawn view and view on the spring of gushing lava cavity there, which is uncommon to see.

The city is prestigious, just like the focal point of Javanese expressive arts and culture, for example, the Wayang Kulit shadow puppetry, just as for music, artful dance, show, verse, and batik. Home to many captivating attractions and two UNESCO Heritage Sites, Yogyakarta is something beyond a social and strict site.

Yogyakarta is one of the most enjoyable cities in Southeast Asia, in spite of the fact that you might never have heard of it before now. Make sure to take day trips from Yogyakarta to Borobudur or Prambanan (or both, if possible!) to round out your Yogyakarta itinerary.

2. Ubud

Known as Bali's craft and culture capital, Ubud is a definitive spot to appreciate different customary exhibitions, from the infamous Kecak fire dance to nearby adolescents rehearsing their gamelan in the city center. You can get one of these exhibitions anyplace from the Royal Palace to eateries and public spots.

The Ubud Monkey Forest, situated on focal Ubud's edges, is home to more than 700 since quite a while ago followed macaques. This regular safe-haven is maybe the most popular in Bali because of its local area based administration, area, and simple entry.

Administered by the Padangtegal town, Ubud Monkey Forest is a logical exploration position and a site of profound and social perspectives, as neighborhood residents purify consecrated sanctuaries. The Ubud Monkey Forest is also called the Sacred Monkey Forest of Padangtegal, and, by its authority assignment, Mandala Wisata Wenara Wana.

1. Derawan Island

2. This archipelago in East Kalimantan is probably the best of tropical heaven, involved six unique islands and some more modest islets, each with its own experiences and appeal. Maratua Island, for instance, is known for its heavenly ocean caverns, lakes, and sumptuous hotels. Kakaban Island offers swimming in a lake loaded with stingless jellyfish. Sangalaki Island is well known for jumping and swimming because of its flourishing underwater scene, loaded up with coral, manta beams, turtles, and that's just the beginning. The generally far off area helps save this archipelago's common magnificence, making it unblemished and wonderful island heaven in Indonesia.

3. Wae Rebo

This small and isolated village was recognized for its rebuilding of the traditional Mbaru Niang traditional house based on the spirit of community cooperation towards a sustainable tradition, while at the same time improving its village welfare. Wae Rebo is a small, very out of the way village.

- **LINGKO SPIDER WEB RICE FIELDS - WALKING TOURS**
- The most stunning perspective over some of these fields is offered at Cara Village arranged on a little slope 17km west of Ruteng in Cancar. With their round, spider trap structure, these parcels are remarkable eye-catchers in Manggarai.

8. Malaysia

There are a lot of great nations on the planet. It is because that Malaysia is uncommon among great countries on the earth. Malaysia is unique on account of the variety of races, religions, and societies. Because of the variety, Malaysian produces a remarkable component that different nations don't have. Malaysia is known for its lovely seashores, separated islands, raised slope stations, and UNESCO World Heritage Sites.

1. Selangor

Selangor portrays Malaysia's generally evolved and populated state that paves the way to Kuala Lumpur's never-ending suburbia.

Selangor is occupied with so much amazing and interesting things; shopping centers spread in numerous ways. At the point when you can't shop in any way, shape, or form shop any longer, head to the close by Genting Highlands — Malaysia's variant of Vegas roosted on top of a mountain. The First World Hotel and Plaza is the world's most prominent inn with 10,500 rooms and an amusement park.

- **Malaysia Agriculture Park, Shah Alam**
- This 1,258ha park is the biggest agroforestry park on the planet, containing tests of practically every rural asset in the country, including oil and coconut palms, padi fields, organic product trees, and elastic trees all set in a rainforest. Through various outside displays, live showings, nature trails, and a large group of instructive projects, guests are offered unmatched freedoms to find out about and make the most of Malaysia's rich characteristic ascribes. Different attractions here incorporate two dams, a fishing lake, a mild house, an engineered overpass, and a winged creature and safari park. Bikes are accessible available inside the recreation center. Spending chalets are likewise accessible.

1. Tanah Rata

The little town of Tanah Rata is the standard base for spending voyagers wishing to investigate Malaysia's delightful Cameron Highlands. With temperatures that plunge as low as 50 F around evening time, Tanah Rata is an invited break from Southeast Asia's warmth and stickiness.

Straightforward, green tea estates sticking to the encompassing slopes and never-ending blossoming blossoms loan a sweet smell to the air. The peacefulness of the landscape is infectious; Tanah Rata's vibe is charmingly loose, and individuals are benevolent. Wilderness strolls anticipate the daring while strawberry ranches and rich nurseries engage those wishing to remain nearer to progress.

Cameron Highlands Discover The History

In the event that you are around Cameron and need to find out about its set of experiences, at that point visit the Cameron Highlands Discover The History that includes a portion of the important photos and antiquities with respect to Cameron. The shows are worked by the retreat that houses the display space. You can remain there to have an intensive admittance to the antique highlights that are captivating and will make you nostalgic about the bygone eras. There are loads of highlights that will cause you to think back on your adolescence. The best feature of the display is the Time Tunnel through which you can investigate the historical backdrop of Cameron. The displays are interesting to individuals of all age gatherings and you can visit here with your family just as companions.

1.Kuala Lumpur

KL is broadly perceived for various milestones, including Petronas Twin Towers (the world's tallest twin high rises), Petaling Street swap meet, and Batu Caves, which is more than 400 million years ago. Kuala Lumpur is the capital city of Malaysia, flaunting shining high rises, provincial design, enchanting local people, and a horde of characteristic attractions. Separated into various areas, its principle center is known as the Golden Triangle which contains Bukit Bintang, KLCC and Chinatown.

- Menara KL Tower
- Remaining on the Bukit Nanas Forest Reserve, the 421m-high KL Tower is now the world's fifth tallest design. Authoritatively known as Menara KL, it has been eclipsed by the Petronas Twin Towers however stays a significant structural marker and flaunts excellent perspectives on the city. The survey deck is in any event 100 meters higher than the Petronas Tower's Skybridge - to get free tickets make sure to show up before the expected time.

1. Taman Negara

In a real sense, Taman Negara signifies "public park" in Malaysia, and well, that is the thing that it is! Taman Negara is Malaysia's most established public park and is viewed as one of the world's most established tropical rainforests. A long shade walkway allows guests to see life high in the trees that regularly isn't obvious starting from the earliest stage.

You can appreciate cascades and wonderful journeying, fowl spots, boating, fishing, night safaris, and there's even an opportunity to see wild elephants — in case you're lucky. Vacationers rest across the waterway in Kuala Tahan and afterward take modest boats to the recreation center passage. Some genuinely guided journeying is accessible in Taman Negara, as is surrendering.

11. Thailand

Situated in southern Asia it is known for extraordinary food, hand to hand fighting, sea shores, and numerous sanctuaries. Thailand likewise has numerous islands that are notable that have various retreats for sightseers. On the off chance that you have ever eaten Thai food, you'll know it's a remunerating experience.

Thailand is home to natural life in its numerous public parks, seashores, and rocky territory. In the south, there are whole sea shores loaded up with monkeys, with travelers rushing to places like Monkey Beach on Koh Phi to perceive beauty.

1. Bangkok

generally acclaimed for its loved nightlife scene and cheerful climate, this is the place where 99%, everything being equal, will end up at any rate once when in Bangkok. It is additionally a convenience focal point for some as an incredible assortment of modest convenience types can be found inside the region of Khao San Road. Bangkok, Thailand's capital is an enormous city known for its resplendent hallowed places and energetic road life. The boat-filled Chao Phraya River takes care of its channels, streaming past the Rattanakosin imperial area, home to extravagant Grand Palace and its sacrosanct Wat Phra Kaew Temple. Close by is Wat Pho Temple with a huge leaning back Buddha and, on the contrary shore, Wat Arun Temple with its lofty advances and Khmer-style tower.

On the off chance that you like shopping you need to look at this spot. In the event that you scorn shopping you need to give this spot a wide compartment. With more than 8000 slows down covering 27 sections of land of room this is perhaps the biggest market on the planet.

Open each Saturday and Sunday it draws in almost 200,000 guests per day, you will discover all that you might envision available to be purchased here and generally at nearby costs instead of traveler costs, it is unquestionably worth getting a guide before you go to maintain a strategic distance from you being lost on the lookout for quite a long time.

2. Pai

Pai essentially blossoms with the travel industry. Generally, it is the most attractive and amazing place to visit for tourists. Notable among explorers for its casual climate, the town is brimming with modest guesthouses, gift shops, and cafés. In the environs of the town are spas and elephant camps.

The best activities in Pai Thailand are outside of what might be expected and not your customary Thai vacation destinations. I like to consider it the 'Pai opening' in light of the fact that once you show up; you will not have any desire to leave. I initially came to Pai for five days and wound up leaving a half year later... It resembles you're stuck on an island, simply less the sea shore and add mountains, wilderness, cascades and natural aquifers.

Pai is the sort of spot you expect to remain for a couple of evenings and wind up leaving a month later, that is its excellence. The best activities in Pai are only a short motorbike ride away, so bounce on that bicycle and investigate for yourself.

3. Khao Sok

Khao Sok is truly perhaps the most dazzling spots I've ever been on my travel. The tones, the scenes, the crudeness – it's an uncommon spot. It's home to uncommon species, for example, the goliath parasitic Rafflesia bloom, hornbill flying creatures, gibbons, and tigers. The recreation center can be enjoyed by elephant-back safari, climbing trail, and pontoon, kayak, or kayak employing the Sok stream.

Khao Sok National Park is situated in the South of Thailand. Envision lakes, limestone mountains, rainforests (and parasites), and breathtaking perspectives. It's a well-known objective because there are numerous Khao Sok exercises each explorer ought to do while in Thailand.

4. Sukhothai

The bubbling of culture in this city during the thirteenth and fourteenth hundreds of years CE has left a permanent engraving on Thai workmanship, language, and governmental issues, and Sukhothai is as yet venerated as the origin of Thai culture by Thais today. Further abroad in the northern zone, the overwhelming brilliant 36 foot Buddha at Wat Si Chum is well worth seeing. Access to each zone costs around 100 baht and bikes can be leased from the fundamental doors for under 50 baht each day.

A little city in northern Thailand, Sukhothai is a well-known traveler objective because of the close by relics of an old town by a similar name. Noteworthy Sukhothai was the primary capital of Thailand, at that point, Siam, during the thirteenth century. Numerous sanctuaries, castles, and landmarks from this period can be found in the Sukhothai Historical Park.

The recreation center is partitioned into various zones, with each highlighting a few exhumed sanctuaries, chedis, Buddha figures, and different landmarks with noteworthy plaster reliefs. Wat Mahathat is viewed as the most incredible sanctuary with its standing Buddha relics and lotus-formed stupa. In the recreation center is Wat Si Chum's structure, which houses an enormous 50-foot tall sitting Buddha.

CONCLUSION

Life is full of so many opportunities and adventures, while it depends on the person who is willing to take risk and do so much in life, if you do not take stance right now how you will know the unparalleled beauty around the world, or wander what you have missed in life. Life gives do much chances and it is on us how we take them granted for ourselves.

world is full of places and sites which we cannot even imagine in life but are worth seeing and now I have given you the opportunity to see the glimpse of world here and now up to you now, how you enjoy yourselves in 2021 after so much troubles and tragedies.

The Top 9+1 North America Destinations for family and Co.

Everything you need to know to travel North America on a Budget with your family and make your dream holiday become reality in 2021.

BY

The lost Traveler.

Contents

America

The USA is one of those countries which is third most visited country on the planet. Yet, we are specific, and numerous individuals are pondering, "for what reason would you like to go to the USA?" Even though it seems like everybody has a deep understanding of the United States of America, it's as yet a country that will shock you once you initially go there. Merely attempting to find out about it is a valid justification for visiting. There are all kinds of fun exercises, numerous delightful scenes and various societies living respectively. It's a gigantic country, and you should go more than once if you genuinely need to have the entire American experience. Anyway, we can promise you, visiting the States won't be exhausting by any means. The nation is very decidedly ready for the vacationers. Everywhere in the country, you will see there is a great deal of security. It very well may be somewhat exhausting now and then, however toward the end, it is ideal. That way, you can be looser and not all the time thinking about the case you're protected or not. The administrations are likewise extraordinary, regardless of if it's extravagance or modest travel. They will consistently treat you very well at inns, cafés. But in any case, on the off chance that you don't care to set up the excursion without anyone else, you could generally do it with an office, which, there are thousands that arrangement outings to the States.

1. Wailea, Hawaii

What is the best North American island get-away? Indeed, it's a city so pleasant, you picked it twice. Wailea, clearly, is never the bridesmaid, consistently the lady. Favored with five shocking bow formed sea shores, richly in vogue resorts, and close by Ahihi-Kinau Normal Region Save, this location spoils voyagers' faculties with a-list food, delightful sights, new sea aromas, and welcoming climate.

2. Cambria, California

Sitting on seemingly the prettiest stretch of waterfront land in California, Cambria is an untainted little town among massive excellence. Reflecting such merits, it bounced from No. 6 to No. 2 this year. Walk the Moonstone Sea shore Footpath to spot ocean life, or take a horseback visit through the mountains with Covell's California Clydesdales. Frequently filling in as headquarters for those venturing out to Hearst Mansion, Cambria has a lot charms to investigate!

3. Springdale, Utah

Remaining emphatically in the No. 3 spot, Springdale draws in guests who like experience, excellence, and nature. This is the spot to remain while investigating Zion Public Park to see the becoming flushed tons of sandstone precipices. The town is a top pick for its town like appeal, southern Utah scene, and well-disposed local area.

4. Ashland, Oregon

In nearness to the Rebel Waterway—and facilitating top notch theater and the amazing Shakespeare Celebration—Ashland advances to craftsmanship sweethearts and open air lovers the same. Balance a day of trail running, stream boating, or skiing with asparagus dumpling soup or smoked brisket with stew sauce at Child. Or on the other hand, go through the day shopping neighborhood stores, at that point treat yourself to a loosening up night with the Rebel Valley Orchestra.

5. Sedona, Arizona

Sedona is an enchanted place, but it took no fairy dust to jet it up from No. 20 this year. With its outdoor beauty, calming retreats and spas, and highly walkable downtown, the appeal is undeniable. Unreal starry skies are the reason for a night hike on Baldwin Trailhead, and Gallery Row is the spot for an afternoon of culture.

6. Cambridge, Massachusetts

A city of neighborhoods, Cambridge invites you to pick your favorite flavor. Harvard Square is the most compact and will be favored by book lovers, but Central Square packs a lot into a small space, and is an ideal area to explore the eclectic flavors of the city. Head to East Cambridge for hidden gems, or super-cute Inman Square for thrift shopping and beer sipping.

7. Minneapolis, Minnesota

Up two slots this year, Minneapolis rounds out our top 10 vacation spots in North America, and continues to gain popularity. Historically underestimated, this Minnesota city has been catching attention for its friendly people, international and regional foods (we'll take a Jucy Lucy, please), beautiful natural surroundings, and entertainment options. Sports enthusiasts will find plenty to love, as the city boasts five pro teams.

8. Paso Robles, California

Generally known for wine, Paso Robles dominates at more than reds and whites. The region has seen an ascent in cideries, refineries, and breweries. Pair your ideal refreshment with a similarly extraordinary feast at diners in and out of town. Take your pick of flavors, from California coast-meets-Mexico at Fish Gaucho to nearby joys at Thomas Slope Organics..

9. Solvang, California

This Danish town is encircled by activities. Wine sampling, horseback riding, theater going, climbing, cake snacking—the rundown is perpetual. Respect the engineering, windmills, and Little Mermaid form, and on the off chance that you love celebrations, come for occasions like Solvang Danish Days or Taste of Solvang.

10.   Bar Harbor, Maine

New to the Top 50 this year, Bar Harbor's lucky number is clearly 13. What could have catapulted the city onto the list of best places to vacation? Well, Cadillac Mountain and Acadia National Park might have a little something to do with it, but museums, lighthouses, breweries, and music festivals (to name a few), appeal to curious visitors and keep them coming back.

11.   Key West, Florida

Key West has been a perennial favorite and beloved vacation spot for its array of appealing attractions. SCUBA and snorkeling, famous bars like Sloppy Joe's, parks, ecotours, beaches, celebrated pie, and daily sunset festivals greet happy travelers. Warm winter temperatures keep it a go-to for escaping frosty weather.

12.   Sanibel, Florida

Not to be too outdone by its southerly state-mate, Sanibel clinches the No. 15 spot in its first appearance. Visitors fall in love with the place for many reasons. Go shelling on the beach, fill up on fresh seafood at joints like the super-fun Bubble Room, and spend peaceful time at J.N. Ding Darling National Wildlife Refuge.

13.   Pittsburgh, Pennsylvania

Pittsburgh continues to rise in estimation, offering visitors gems like the Andy Warhol Museum, the Butterfly Garden at Phipps Conservatory, foodie tours, thrilling sports teams, and many remarkable neighborhoods to explore. As a riverfront city, Pittsburgh provides scenic paths, trails, and opportunities to get on the water. Who knew Pittsburgh was one of the best places to vacation? Our reviewers did!

14.　　Washington, D.C.

Go to a walk or study the country's set of experiences — D.C. these days is perhaps the best spot to go for both. Come see the cherry blooms and dream of sunnier occasions. Or on the other hand look at the exuberant nightlife and let loose a little. Numerous free exhibition halls, remembrances, occasions, and exercises will fill your days without purging your pockets.

15.   Charleston, South Carolina

Charleston winds up on such countless top choices records, it ought to get its own image bargain. Workmanship, culture, entertainment, unwinding — this city dominates at each. Go on a mobile visit to take everything in, or pick from five territory sea shores to investigate. Food is a significant feature of city culture, and South Carolina has the merchandise, so come hungry.

16.   Rosemont, Illinois

Travelers love to stay in Rosemont, a welcoming village just outside of Chicago. Jumping two spots this year, it continues to be a high-rated location. Maybe it's the friendly residents, maybe enthusiastic Wolves fans are casting their votes, or maybe it's just the perfect place to escape city crowds. Whatever the reason, people are crushing on Rosemont.

17.   Durango, Colorado

Up from the 40th slot last year, Durango impressed 2017 travelers with awe-inspiring nature, laid-back locals, Old West vibes, and plenty of cultural pursuits. Visit one of the many galleries or museums, like the Animas Museum, which highlights Durango history. The outdoors tempts explorers with all the things to see and do in the San Juan National Forest and beyond.

18.   Kihei, Hawaii

Hawaiian eminence of yesteryear decided to relax in Kihei, and with its radiant climate and lovely sea shore sees, you realize those royals had the correct thought. The typical beachy suspects—swimming, swimming, surfing—sparkle a little more splendid in this southern Maui city, and come winter, you may detect a humpback whale from shore.

19.   Lahaina, Hawaii

Life is truly rainbows and sunbeams in Lahaina. Situated near the West Maui mountains, the city sees a near-daily "5 o'clock rainbow" that stretches across the valley. Visit the largest banyan tree in the U.S., indulge in the best nightlife on Maui, and peruse the galleries along Front Street; your time in Lahaina can be as eclectic as the rainbows are colorful.

20.   Lihue, Hawaii

The Hawaii love-fest continues for Lihue. Perhaps the nectars at Koloa Rum Company have magical properties, or the beauty of Wailua Falls casts a potent spell; whatever sorcery graces Lihue, we're all in. If you can tear yourself away from the beach, go to the Kauai Museum to learn about the history and formation of this bewitching island.

21.   Chicago, Illinois

Chicago's history is closely tied to its proximity to Lake Michigan. While the Chicago River historically handled much of the region's waterborne cargo, today's huge lake freighters use the city's Lake Calumet Harbor on the South Side. The lake also provides another positive effect: moderating Chicago's climate, making waterfront neighborhoods slightly warmer in winter and cooler in summer.

22.   Asheville, North Carolina

Asheville is a major hub of whitewater recreation, particularly whitewater kayaking, in the eastern US. Many kayak manufacturers have their bases of operation in the Asheville area. Some of the most distinguished whitewater kayakers live in or around Asheville. In its July/August 2006 journal, the group American Whitewater named Asheville one of the top five US whitewater cities. Asheville is also home to numerous Disc Golf courses. Soccer is another popular recreational sport in Asheville. There are two youth soccer clubs in Asheville, Asheville Shield Football Club and HFC. The Asheville Hockey League provides opportunities for youth and adult inline hockey at an outdoor rink at Carrier Park. The rink is open to the public and pick-up hockey is also available. The Asheville Civic Center has held recreational ice hockey leagues in the past.

23. Moab, Utah

Since the 1970s, tourism has played an increasing role in the local economy. Partly due to the John Ford movies, partly due to magazine articles, the area has become a favorite of photographers, <u>rafters</u>, hikers, <u>rock climbers</u>, and most recently <u>mountain bikers</u>. Moab is also an increasingly popular destination for <u>four-wheelers</u> as well as for <u>BASE jumpers</u> and those rigging <u>highlining</u>, who are allowed to practice their sport in the area. About 16 miles (26 km) south of Moab is <u>Hole N" The Rock</u>, a 5,000-square-foot (460 m²) 14-room home carved into a rock wall which *National Geographic* has ranked as one of the top 10 <u>roadside attractions</u> in the United States. Moab's population swells temporarily in the spring and summer months with the arrival of numerous people employed seasonally in the outdoor recreation and tourism industries.

24. Seattle, Washington

Seattle is situated between the saltwater Puget Sound (an arm of the Pacific Sea) toward the west and Lake Washington toward the east. The city's central harbor, Elliott Inlet, is essential for Puget Sound, which makes the city a maritime port. Toward the west, past Puget Sound, are the Kitsap Landmass and Olympic Mountains on the Olympic Promontory; toward the east, past Lake Washington and the Eastside rural areas, are Lake Sammamish and the Course Reach. Lake Washington's waters stream to Puget Sound through the Lake Washington Boat Channel (comprising of two man-made trenches, Lake Association, and the Hiram M. Chittenden Locks at Salmon Cove, finishing off with Shilshole Straight on Puget Sound).

25.   Chandler, Arizona

There are numerous properties in the town of Chandler which are considered to be historical and have been included either in the National Register of Historic Places or listed as such by the Chandler Historical Society. The Historic McCullough-Price House, a 1938 Pueblo Revival-style home, was donated to the city by the Price-Propstra family in 2001. The city renovated and opened it to the public in 2007. On June 12, 2009, the McCullough-Price House was added to the National Register of Historic Places, the official listing of America's historic and cultural resources worthy of preservation. The city of Chandler operates the facility, which is located southwest of Chandler Fashion Center at 300 S. Chandler Village Dr.

26.   Boston, Massachusetts

In the core of the city is Boston Normal, America's most seasoned park and the beginning of the Opportunity Trail. In this huge green space, which is abundantly utilized by local people all year, are different landmarks and the Focal Covering Ground of 1756. You can lease skates to use on the Frog Lake from November through mid-Walk, appreciate the spring blooms and fall foliage colors reflecting in its surface, and in summer, watch adolescents sprinkle about in the swimming pool. Abutting it on the west side of Charles Road, is the 24-section of land Public Nursery, America's most seasoned greenhouse, just as Victorian-style landmarks and sculptures, including an equestrian sculpture of George Washington and mainstream current bronzes of a group of ducks deified in Robert McCloskey's youngsters' book Clear A path for the Ducklings. One of Boston's most notable encounters for all ages is riding around the lake in the nursery's middle on the acclaimed Swan Boats, first dispatched during the 1870s.

27.　　Cleveland, Ohio

One of the most popular things to do in Cleveland is visit the Rock & Roll Hall of Fame. Designed by I.M. Pei, it is more of an experience than a museum. The history of popular music is spread over six floors in an atmosphere of multimedia exuberance, with such rarities as the manuscript of *Purple Haze*, written by Jimi Hendrix. It is here that the rock and roll music industry honors its finest entertainers.Music enthusiasts could spend days going through all the museum has to offer, with permanent exhibitions and traveling national and international shows. The eye-catching, state-of-the-art building sits on the shores of Lake Erie. The best way to experience the museum is to start on Level 0, where you find the Hall of Fame Inductees, and work your way to the top.

28.　　New Orleans, Louisiana

The French Quarter of New Orleans is what most tourists come to see when they visit the city. Set along a bend on the Mississippi River, the main attraction here is the architecture, but it is also a great area for dining and entertainment. The old buildings, some of which date back 300 years, show French influences, with arcades, wrought iron balconies, red-tiled roofs, and picturesque courtyards. Many of these buildings now contain hotels, restaurants, souvenir shops, galleries, and a profusion of jazz spots with entertainment of varying quality. The most famous street in the French Quarter is **Bourbon Street**, but it is not necessarily the highlight of the area. This street is relatively benign by day but at night transforms into a loud and boisterous pedestrian area that may not always feel safe. **Royal Street** offers a great mix of history, fine cuisine, and unique shopping opportunities, with some higher end stores, galleries, and hotels. One of the notable buildings on Royal Street is the Court of Two Sisters (1832), now a restaurant known for its jazz brunch. To hear some quality musicians playing traditional jazz music, **Frenchmen Street** is the place to go. Good restaurants can also be found along here, and artists frequent the area. Also, not to be missed in the French Quarter are **Jackson Square** and **St Louis**

Cathedral, located just off the waterfront. Buskers, musicians, and artists set up around the square.

29.   Treasure Island, Florida

Fortune Island's most popular fascination is our sea shore which is comprised of three miles of white sandy sea shore lined by the wonderful Bay of Mexico. You can stroll along the coastline or go for a walk on the Fortune Island Sea shore Trail. Other Fortune Island exercises incorporate remote oceans fishing contracts, parasailing, boat rentals or essentially laying in the sun on Fortune Island sea shore. The Fortune Island Sea shore Trail is a mile long walkway along the east side of the sea shore. The Fortune Island Sea shore Trail gives simple admittance to the inns, eateries and bars that make up the core of Fortune Island's inn area. Fortune Island's midtown gives a few apparel stores, a pharmacy, banks, alcohol store, flower vendor, cafés, bars and soon another supermarket. John's Pass Town borders the north finish of Fortune Island while St. Pete Sea shore toward the south has an enormous number of stores, cafés and bars. St. Petersburg is toward the east of Fortune Island and brags of Significant Group Baseball and a bustling midtown region.

30.   Park City, Utah

Utah Olympic Park was the home of several events during the 2002 Winter Olympics, and is still an official training site for current and future Olympic athletes. Admission to the park and several of the park's attractions are free, including the Alf Engen Ski Museum, the Eccles Salt Lake 2002 Olympic Winter Games Museum, the Discovery Zone obstacles course, the Mountain Challenge course and several hiking trails. For a once-in-a-lifetime experience, visitors can ride with a professional driver on the signature Comet Bobsled to feel the same g-force and blazing speed that Olympic competitors enjoy. Other activities – all priced individually – include three levels of climbing and ropes tours, a zip line and a one-hour guided tour that visits the world's highest Nordic ski jumps.

31.   Fargo, North Dakota

Across state lines in Moorhead, Minnesota, and a mile walk from downtown Fargo, the Hjemkomst Center is home to the Historical and Cultural Society of Clay County. At the facility, the **Hopperstad Stave Church** replica and the sailable **Hjemkomst Viking Ship** attract the most visits and are both tangible icons of the Norwegian history of the area.Several permanent and rotating exhibits pertaining to the county are maintained by the historical society. The Hjemkomst Center also hosts various special events throughout the year, including a German Kulturfest and the Scandinavian Hjemkomst & Midwest Viking Festival.

32.   Henderson, Nevada

Lake Las Vegas, a man-made lake located in Henderson, stretches for 320 acres. Visitors can utilize the lake for fishing, sailing and swimming. A host of facilities surround the lake as well, including hotels, spas and golf courses. Situated on the shores of the lake, guests find the MonteLago Village Resort, a Mediterranean-inspired area filled with shops, restaurants, cafes and cobblestone streets. Lake Las Vegas remains a popular destination for business meetings and trade shows. The lake region also plays host to a series of concerts and festivals throughout the year.

33.　　Garden Grove, California

Atlantis Park is one of the best loved green spots in the city of Garden Grove and is a great place to come if you are travelling with younger visitors. There are a number of grassy knolls in the park as well as play areas for children, and one of the signature attractions in the park is the dragon slide that takes the form of a large sea serpent.

You will also find a range of concrete animals that children can ride as well as climbers and swings that mean that little ones will never be bored.

34.   Scottsdale, Arizona

Taliesin West was the winter home of architect Frank Lloyd Wright and is today the headquarters of the **Frank Lloyd Wright Foundation** and the School of Architecture at Taliesin West. Students transition between Taliesin in Wisconsin and Taliesin West in Scottsdale, spending summers in the north and winters in the south, same as they have been doing for decades. This campus is a fascinating insight into the genius of this famous architect. The buildings have seen ongoing changes and have been restored to their former look and feel. Tours are mandatory if you want to see the property, but guides are passionate about telling the story of the site and provide interesting insights without overwhelming you with details. You can learn about the concepts the architect employed in the buildings and gain a better understanding of what you are seeing on the tour. Taliesin West is a working architecture school, and you may see students hard at work on their drafting tables if you visit during the winter. The tours take place inside and outside. One of the requirements of students is to create their own simple dwelling out in the desert, where they live while they're here.

35.   Estes Park, Colorado

Getting off the road and onto the trail in an ATV is a classic Colorado experience. Estes Park ATV Rentals offers unguided ATV and other vehicle rentals, so you can explore at your own pace and not be hindered by a group - and the views around here are simply stunning.

The ATVs come with maps, helmets, and gas and are already parked on the trail, so you don't need to bring anything except your driver's license. You can book a half- or a full-day rental.

36.　Santa Fe, New Mexico

The Historical center of New Mexico Complex houses four galleries that investigate the state's legacy. The New Mexico History Historical center narratives the state's set of experiences from the sixteenth century onwards via displays that take a gander at the local populaces, colonization, and the manners in which the St Nick Fe Trail formed the state's economy and improvement. The exhibition hall is housed in The Royal residence of Lead representatives, the previous seventeenth century seat of the Spanish government, which is a Public Notable Milestone. Guests can visit this adobe royal residence and see rooms total with period furniture, set up as they would have been during the 1600s. Royal residence Press offers an exceptional opportunity to see live exhibits of the principal print machine in the province of New Mexico. One more fascination at the complex incorporates the Fight Angelico Chavez History Library, which contains chronicled materials and notable records, and the Photograph Documents, where guests will discover in excess of 750,000 pictures that date back similar to the mid-nineteenth century. The complex likewise has a Local American expressions market that works day by day.

37.   Arlington, Virginia

Located at the back entrance to Arlington National Cemetery, the United States Marine Corps War Memorial is a military monument dedicated to the memory of all the members of the United States Marine Corps who have died defending the country since 1775. It is also known as the Iwo Jima Memorial. The memorial is based on a famous photograph taken by Joe Rosenthal: it depicts the raising of the American flag on Mount Suribachi during the Battle of Iwo Jima in World War II. The massive sculpture was designed by Horace W. Peaslee and the sculpture was completed by Felix de Weldon.

38.   Laguna Beach, California

At the intersection of Broadway Street and the Pacific Coast Highway, Main Beach Park is an iconic oceanfront destination complete with sand volleyball nets, a boardwalk, and lifeguards on duty. Popular for celebrities and average tourists alike, the beach area gives a certain vibe that just feels like Southern California, especially come sunset when the surrounding hillsides full of mansions seem to glow. Riptides are present just offshore, and those interested in swimming should consult with the lifeguards first. A central attraction of Laguna Beach, Main Beach Park branches in either direction for more beautiful sights to see. Plenty of local shops and restaurants of Laguna Beach are inland from the park, including the local favorite, Nick's Laguna Beach.

39.   Newport, Rhode Island

Since it was built in 1852 for William S. Wetmore, Chateau-Sur-Mer has gone through so many reconstructions that today, it is a catalog of nearly all the major Victorian architectural and decorative styles. The Wetmore, whose fortune stemmed from the China Trade, came early to Newport, when it was the retreat of wealthy families of culture and intellect. Their well-traveled son, who was enthusiastic about the Arts & Crafts movement, hired Richard Morris Hunt to renovate and enlarge the house, and Hunt made it into a showcase for the geometric Eastlake style. The library and dining room bear the stamp of their later Italian designer, and an upstairs sitting room was inspired by Turkish motifs. Perhaps the most remarkable architectural feature is the soaring 45-foot central hall with stained-glass skylights.

40.   Palm Desert, California

Escape the heat of the desert with a quick ride into the mountains on the Palm Springs Aerial Tramway. Standing on the edge of Palm Springs, Mount San Jacinto rises more than 10,000 feet above the desert floor and can be easily accessed with a ride on the scenic tramway. The tramway, which opened in 1963, has the world's largest rotating aerial tram cars. The cars are suspended from cables, like a ski lift, and the cables are strung atop metal towers installed on the mountainside. From the top, the view out over the desert is fantastic, and on hot days, the cool air (sometimes 30 to 40 degrees lower than that at the desert floor) can be a refreshing treat. During the winter, there is snow at the top. In less than 10 minutes, the tram will take you up Chino Canyon to an elevation of 8,500 feet. At the top, called the Mountain Station, there are observation decks, two restaurants, historical displays, and videos on the construction of the tram. From here, 50 miles of hiking trails run through the pine forests of the Santa Rosa and San Jacinto Mountains National Monument.

41.   Avalon, California

Part of the Channel Islands, Santa Catalina lies about 22 miles southwest of Los Angeles. The island is a popular destination with boaters and day trippers. Avalon is the main population center and where most of the action is centered. On the other end of the island is the much smaller village of Two Harbors. While most people come to Santa Catalina Island to wander around and enjoy a day of leisure, other popular things to do include glass bottom boat tours, scuba diving, kayaking, and parasailing. You can reach the island by ferry from San Pedro, Long Beach, Newport Beach, and Dana Point.

42.   Bozeman, Montana

In Bozeman, it's hard to miss the collegiate "M" posted high onto the ridgeline of **Bridger Canyon**. This 250-foot white-rock letter was built piece by piece by students of Montana State University in 1915 and has since served as a pride point for the University and a symbol for the city. This decorative door hanger at the mouth of Bridger Canyon is more than just aesthetically pleasing though, and two short hiking trails encourage visitors to hike up and enjoy the view. Two hiking trails lead up to the "M" and adjacent sitting benches. At the trailhead, the steeper half-mile trail forks to the right, and the 1.5-mile switchback trail heads left. Both trails gain 850 feet to reach the "M", which provides straining legs for most average hikers. The "M" is just an introduction to Bozeman hiking endeavors. Alongside many other natural areas in the region, the "M" trail is just the beginning of the 20-mile **Bridger Foothills National Scenic Trail**.

43.   La Jolla, California

The spectacular La Jolla Underwater Park promises a wonderful adventure and is one of the top La Jolla attractions. Home to a natural marine life preservation and aquatic recreation zone, it sprawls over 6,000 acres of shoreline and shallow tidelands between Ellen Browning Scripps Park and La Jolla Shores. This incredible ecological reserve hosts two artificial reefs, two underwater canyons, and a vast kelp forest, creating a pristine and protected marine habitat in which a variety of oceanic flora and fauna live. Two sunken artificial reefs attract marine life close to shore and make conditions perfect for swimming and snorkeling in the crisp waters, teeming with beautiful sea creatures. Visitors can take part in a wonderful scuba diving adventure beyond the reefs in the 600-foot deep La Jolla Canyon where migrating whales are often spotted. The La Jolla Underwater Park is a protected zone and fishing is prohibited. However, other water-based activities such as kayaking, swimming, snorkeling and scuba diving are popular pastimes in the reserve.

44.   Portland, Maine

The collection at the Portland Museum of Art features fine and decorative arts dating from the 1700s onward. The museum's collections focus on American and European paintings, and also include a variety of other media like sculpture, pottery, furniture, and other creations, housing more than 18,000 works. This includes 650-plus works by Winslow Homer, including oil paintings, etchings, and watercolor. Those interested in visiting the nearby Winslow Homer House can purchase tickets at the museum. The museum is also home to the works of major artists including Cassat, Renoir, Monet, Degas, Picasso, and O'Keefe. It also hosts special exhibits, rotates its expansive collection regularly, and features spotlight exhibitions of Maine artists. The museum also offers family events and activities, as well as lectures and curator talks.

45. Biloxi, Mississippi

Harrah's has established its brand as a quality casino and accommodation destination, and Harrah's Gulf Coast maintains this reputation in standout fashion. Harrah's Gulf Coast has it all in one package—so much more than just a hotel, the resort includes a large casino, pool and spa, several dining options, and even a concert venue. Known as the Great Lawn, this venue faces the coastline and provides an all-ages-welcome space for musical performances by well-known acts each Saturday night. In addition to all this, Harrah's also has its own 18-hole golf course, which was designed by legend of the sport Jack Nicklaus.

Canada

Canada is blessed to have some tremendous urban communities spread across its colossal land. Winnipeg is known for its reasonableness; Calgary is famous because it's the nearest significant center to Banff National Park; Ottawa is home to fascinating exhibition halls and the Rideau Canal Yellowknife is the funding to visit to see the Northern Lights.

At that point, you have Vancouver, which is undoubtedly the most exciting city in Canada. It expertly mixes metropolitan city existence with its common environmental factors, so you can go from the workplace to the mountains in under 60 minutes. Toronto is the fourth most fabulous city in North America, while Montreal and Quebec City bring European appeal to Canada. Regardless of the cityscape, you are looking for, you'll see it in Canada.

1. Quebec City, Quebec

One of the most beautiful cities in the world, Quebec City beckons travelers with historical sites, captivating views, and rich cultural features. Walk along Dufferin Terrace to ogle Château Frontenac and historic battlefields. Architecture and history buffs will love Place Royale, the spot where the city was founded. Have a quiet moment at Jardin Jeanne d'Arc, a lush park with pristine gardens.

2. Calgary, Alberta

Travelers flock to Calgary for its annual events like the Calgary Stampede, dubbed "The Greatest Outdoor Show on Earth." Whatever your tastes, Calgary has something incredible for you—from the Calgary Folk Music Festival to The Big Taste. Nature is ever-present, too, in the many city parks and, of course, nearby national park superstar, Banff.

3. Victoria, British Columbia

Victoria is a feast of good. The restaurants serve up diverse and delicious choices, the art galleries are filled with interesting works, and the festivals are plentiful and entertaining. Add in easy access to world-renowned Butchart Gardens, as well as many beaches, lakes, and regional parks, and you have a city made for multiple visits. It comes as no surprise it's rated one of the best cities in North America.

4. Montreal, Quebec

Montreal knows how to rack up the accolades, and its honors include being named a UNESCO City of Design. Experience the goods first-hand when you wander the streets—from historical buildings like the Chalet du Mont Royal to modernist Mies Van der Rohe structures. If you're craving some green space, take a breather in the beautiful Mount Royal Park.

5. Vancouver, British Columbia

One of the more famous tourist places in North America, Vancouver is a city so enjoyable it takes the awesome majesty of nearby Whistler and Vancouver Island to tempt people away. Nature aside, urban experiences within Vancouver are some of the best in the world, including the food, art, nightlife, and attractions. Treat yourself at Boulevard Kitchen & Oyster Bar for your first taste, and you'll see what we mean by world-class.

CONCLUSION

Life is full of so many opportunities and adventures, while it depends on the person who is willing to take risk and do so much in life, if you do not take stance right now how you will know the unparalleled beauty around the world, or wander what you have missed in life. Life gives do much chances and it is on us how we take them granted for ourselves. world is full of places and sites which we cannot even imagine in life but are worth seeing and now I have given you the opportunity to see the glimpse of world here and now up to you now, how you enjoy yourselves in 2021 after so much troubles and tragedies.

The Top 9+1 South America Destinations for family and Co.

Everything you need to know to travel South America on a Budget with your family and make your dream holiday become reality in 2021.

BY

The lost Traveler.

TABLE OF CONTENT

1.   Argentina

Argentina is a country loaded with surprises and an extensive rundown of top-notch vacation destinations. The acclaimed Argentina attractions incorporate terrific ice sheets, amazing deserts, beautiful mountains, incredible ocean coasts, and volcanoes. You let you know more in subtleties, and the nation is overflowing with brilliant and energizing social celebrations to current contemporary parties consistently. Diverse customary festivals are loaded with fun exercises that everybody will appreciate, like film seeing in April in Buenos Aires or fair season in February to March. Unquestionably, go to one when visiting Argentina when you need a superior comprehension of their rich culture. Test some typical food and beverages and dance to the beat of traditional music played in the city or gatherings.

1. Iguazu Falls, Argentina

As one of the world's most unbelievable cascades, Iguazu draws more than 1,000,000 guests every year. The UNESCO recorded Iguazu Falls is really many falls that stretch 2 miles (3 km) across the Iguazu Stream. To place the falls into point of view, Iguazu is twice as wide and taller than Niagara Falls. As the cascade crosses the Argentinian and Brazilian boundary, you can visit Iguazu Tumbles from one or the other country. In any case, the most famous sight called the Demon's Throat (Gargantua del Diablo) is in Argentina. Made out of 14 individual cascades, the Demon's Throat is the biggest segment of falls in the entire cascade framework.

There is likewise a walkway to draw near to this noteworthy area. The Brazilian side likewise offers a long walkway driving over the waterway for some fabulous perspectives.

2. Patagonia, Chile & Argentina

Patagonia is a region in southern South America that crosses Chile and Argentina. You can enjoy breathtaking scenery with mountains, glaciers and beautiful lakes of fantastic protected areas. In addition to the fantastic scenery, there are also remnants of ancient cultures, such as cave paintings in the fascinating Cueva de las Manos Pintadas. Some favorite protected areas in the region are the Parque Nacional Torres Del Paine, Parque National Perito Moreno, and Parque Nacional Los Glaciers.

You can find the Parque Nacional Torres Del Paine in southern Chile. As one of the most popular places in Patagonia, there are over 100,000 yearly visitors. The Torres del Paine (Towers of Paine) themselves are granite pillars extending vertically just over 2,000 meters into the sky.

3. Buenos Aires, Argentina

One of the favorite cities for many visitors to South America, Buenos Aires is the capital of Argentina and is where you will enter this fantastic country.

Not simply suited to a brief stop over, in Buenos Aires itself you can find some fantastic nightlife and different things to do. Famously, this is a great place to dance or learn Tango. The first steps to this seductive dance aren't as hard as they look, and there are many beginners' classes to join.

You can also enjoy world-class opera performances, fantastic galleries, theatres, boutique cafes, and of course some excellent restaurants. For many visitors, it's the excellent steaks, wine, and ice cream that are the must try options and there are many different places to dine. Make sure you have a nap, however, as the night-time scene of Buenos Aires is world famous. It's normal here for the nightlife to get going at 3am and even the restaurants are open until late.

4. The Wetlands of Argentina

The Iberá Wetlands are Argentina's answer to the Brazilian Pantanal mentioned farther up. The area is full of lagoons, lakes, and swamps. This is also an important habitat for a wide range of animals and plants.Covering an impressive 7,500 square miles (20,000 km²), the Iberá Wetlands are the world's second largest wetlands after Brazil's Pantanal. These wetlands are not as well-known as the Pantanal or Amazon Rainforest, but offer some incredible sights

Although some of the wildlife has been severely hunted in times gone by, animals are being released back into the area to help the populations recover. You can enjoy exploring the Iberá Wetlands on guided horseback expeditions and boat tours from different ranches. Some of the ranches have been converted into tourist lodges allowing guests to explore this incredible region of Argentina.

5. Mendoza, Argentina

Argentina is the biggest wine maker in South America and one of the biggest around the world. As an extraordinary base for visiting the encompassing grape plantations, Mendoza itself offers an alluring city with a casual vibe where you can appreciate some incredible cafés, shop bistros, and city parks.. The district is liable for creating most of Argentinian wine. As this is Argentina, the fundamental grape assortment developed is Malbec, nonetheless, you can discover a variety of others.

Notwithstanding getting a charge out of the grape plantations, you can appreciate some mind boggling landscape while venturing to every part of the area. Mendoza offers a similar environment as the world's other primary wine developing districts, for example, France, Italy, and California. There is even the Argentinian Wine Course to appreciate and Menoza is a central matter of the schedule.

2. Brazil

Brazil is one of the most significant nations, just as possibly the most various and intriguing country on the planet. The government has quite possibly the most brilliant economies on the earth. This nation is loaded up with a rich portion of history, culture, religion, and incredible games too. With charming individuals, plants, and creatures, this nation is encircled by a fantastic Amazon tropical jungle and perfect tropical seas. Brazil is quite possibly the most exciting vacationer locations for voyagers. Fashion gets the dainty lipped attendant and the cranky storekeeper. Brazilians treat guests as though they were tragically missing companions that they have been holding up their entire lives to get together with once more. The travel industry is a gigantically indispensable area of the nation's economy, and Brazilians try to keep it.

1. Rio de Janeiro, Brazil

One of South America's most well-known urban communities, Rio de Janeiro certainly merit the consideration. Make the most of Rio's renowned and exuberant nature while being near excellent sea shores and unimaginable view. The encompassing mountains give a wonderful background to your visit and the coastline close to Rio is specked with numerous lovely islands.

Notwithstanding the regular excellence, while strolling Rio's roads you will no uncertainty experience music, moving and road parties notable to Rio de Janeiro. There are numerous lodgings that give some amazing perspectives on the city's coastline. Encompassing these, you can discover brilliant eateries, shop bistros, and numerous activities.

2. The Pantanal, Brazil

The Pantanal Wetlands covers a monstrous zone of 140,000 square kilometers (54,000 square miles) and contains a great variety of untamed life. This is an overwhelmed field territory loaded up with untamed life that draws nature darlings the world over. Most of this fantastic biological system is found in Brazil, yet the area likewise crosses into adjoining Paraguay and Bolivia. The Pantanal is regularly where narrative makers film the more magnetic creatures of the Amazon Rainforest, given the higher likelihood of seeing puma, capybara, and others.

Appreciate some inconceivable guided visits across the Pantanal to appreciate delightful perspectives on totally open prairies. The Pantanal gives some incredible perspectives where you can see groups of capybara crossing the fields. Capybara are the world's biggest rat and with webbed feet they are all around adjusted to the wetlands.

3. Brazil's Amazon Rainforest

Brazil contains the biggest part of Amazon Rainforest. You can visit the Brazilian Amazon from Manaus, which is the principle door on the Amazon Stream. Manaus is additionally the biggest city in the Amazon Rainforest. From here, you can investigate the Rio Negro on board some fantastic travels.

Appreciate investigating the Amazon on woodland strolls with your naturalist manage, paddling the streams, and getting a charge out of the two goliath overhang pinnacles of the Cristalino Hotel. You can locate a few distinct monkeys, goliath stream otters, caiman crocodiles, and many various winged creatures.

4. The Cerrado, Brazil

Another lesser-known territory in South America, the Cerrado in Brazil is the country's second biggest living space after the Amazon Rainforest. The Cerrado is a region of dry meadow where you can discover a wide range of creatures. The most adored untamed life sightings here incorporate the rich maned wolves, apparatus utilizing capuchin monkeys, and the jeopardized hyacinth macaw.

This is one of the world's most extravagant savannas. For instance, the Cerrado is home to around 200 distinct vertebrates and around 800 unique fowls. Just as the creature life, more than 40% of all plants in the Cerrado are discovered no place else on Earth. The Cerrado itself is characterized by the dry prairie, contorted trees, and low bushes. You would then be able to appreciate some sensational view on guided visits. This gigantic locale crosses nine states and cover 20% of Brazil. When visiting the territory, appreciate various path to see the untamed life, clear waterways, cascades, and shocking view.

5. The Atlantic Forest, Brazil

The Atlantic Forest along the south-eastern coast of Brazil is one of the world's richest ecosystems but has been severely threatened. A few hundred years ago, this forest covered an area of around 330 million acres (1,300,000 square kilometers). However, after deforestation the Atlantic Forest has been reduced to less than 12% of its former cover.

Despite this, you can find a rich diversity of life here with different trails leading past large trees, wetlands, and rich flora and fauna. The Atlantic Forest is well known among serious birders and there are hundreds of different species to find. These include 200 species found nowhere else on Earth. In addition to birdlife, the forest is home to different monkeys, reptiles and amphibians. When taken together, the species here represent 5% of all the world's vertebrates. Enjoy spotting golden lion tamarins, many different parrots, and the maned three-toed sloth. There is also an abundance of fascinating trees and plants to enjoy.

6. Fernando de Noronha, Brazil

An alluring piece of Brazil, Fernando de Noronha a progression of delightful UNESCO-recorded islands 220 miles (354 km) off the South American coast. The biggest island likewise shares a similar name as the archipelago. Appreciate the ideal tropical island heaven with wonderful sea shores, completely clear water, and a high variety of brilliant fish and other marine life. Fernando de Noronha is the place where you can discover some of most excellent sea shores in Brazil.

There are numerous exercises to appreciate here. This is an extraordinary spot for strolling in the island's timberlands, swimming, and swimming. Appreciate seeing a variety of marine creatures, including one of the world's most elevated centralizations of dolphins, ocean turtles, and numerous brilliant fish.

3.   Peru

Peru has so much more to offer than just a few hot restaurants and well-trod tourist attractions. With landscapes ranging from hidden high-altitude hamlets in the Andes to primordial Amazonian marshes, and enormous sunny beaches to charming colonial towns, not to mention some exciting travel and tourism developments, Peru has quietly transitioned from a top South American travel hotspot to one of the world's most exciting destinations. Here's why you need to go there now.

1. The Amazon River, Peru

The Amazon River is one of the world's largest rivers. Second longest after the Nile, the Amazon is the world's largest river by quantity of water expelled into the Atlantic Ocean. For an example of the river's strength, early sailors could drink fresh water from the Amazon before even sighting land. The Amazon River feeds a rainforest that covers 40% of the South American continent. Being surrounded by wildlife-rich tropical rainforest, the Amazon River is an excellent place for a river cruise.

Our favorite cruise destination is the jungle city of Iquitos in northern Peru. From here, you can explore the beautiful Pacaya Samiria National Reserve. The Pacaya Samiria is Peru's largest national reserve and protects over one million hectares of flooded tropical rainforest. On expeditions from your cruise vessel, enjoy spotting several different monkeys, colorful and iconic toucans, blue and yellow macaws, pink river dolphins, and even find caiman crocodilians while on night cruises.

2. Chan Chan, Peru

The world's biggest adobe city, Chan is situated in the city of Trujillo in northern Peru. Chan was worked by the Chimor Realm that existed between Promotion 900 – 1470. The human progress finished around a similar time as the Inca development was arriving at strength. The Chimor was ultimately crushed by the Inca Realm under the authority of Topa Inca Yupanqui. Chan was once home to more than 50,000 individuals and there are more than 10,000 designs to discover.

Once, these dividers would have held tremendous amounts of gold. In spite of the fact that Chan was vanquished by the Inca, it was the Spanish who plundered the gold from the city. Chimu gold was notable to the Spanish who were currently delivery Incan gold back to Spain. This was the main spot of the Chimor Realm and you can appreciate strolling the roads to see the city and Chan's different fine arts.

3. Lima, Peru

As Peru's capital city, you will initially visit Lima before your excursion to the Consecrated Valley or Amazon Rainforest. Albeit numerous individuals just associate in Lima or stay for one night before their excursion more profound into Peru, Lima can likewise merit a visit for a couple of evenings. One reason is on the grounds that Peruvian cooking is viewed as truly outstanding on the planet. Lima is then lucky to be home to a couple of the world's 50 best food, which you can appreciate on your visit. Lima is likewise wealthy in history and this was from where the Spanish would dispatch Incan gold back to Spain.

Appreciate visiting the interesting Memorable Center to see a considerable lot of the provincial structures. Walk the roads to see famous wooden overhangs and the city from where the Spanish victory of South America was based. Around the principle square, you can see the Court Chairman, Basilica, Government Royal residence, the City Lobby, the Diocese supervisor's Castle, and the intriguing San Francisco Cloister

4. Choquequirao – The Cradle of Gold, Peru

Worked to match Machu Picchu, Choquequirao (the Support of Gold) was thought to have been charged by the Inca Pachacuti's child, Túpac Inca Yupanqui. The construction of Choquequirao is like Machu Picchu and considerably less notable. Choquequirao is likewise thought to have been one of the last fortifications against the Spanish conquistadors. Adding to its verifiable importance, this is thought to have been a political and authoritative center point for the Inca Realm.

Choquequirao is made out of various rooms and structures. You can discover zones saved solely for the Incan tip top, just as various zones for laborers, craftsmans, and the porches and cultivating zones that encompass numerous Incan locales. The site has various designs given to Incan divinities and love. There are territories for the divine beings, for earth, and for water. Albeit a later archeological fascination, and in no way, shape or form also known as Machu Picchu, you can appreciate multi-day climbs to see Choquequirao and even consolidate a trip among Choquequirao and the better known Incan fortress.

5. Huaraz & the Huascarán National Park, Peru

Quite possibly the most visited and appealing pieces of the Andes mountain range, the Huascarán Public Park ensures a zone of the Andes known as the Cordillera Blanca. Inside and encompassing the recreation center, you can locate some lovely glacial masses and tidal ponds. Regardless of whether you're not intrigued by concentrated climbs or hiking, a portion of these can be visited on day climbs from the door city of Huaraz.

The territory secures Mount Huascaran, which is Peru's biggest mountain and gives the public park its name. There are various creatures and plants to see around the recreation center, including the renowned vicuñas. These are the antiquated precursors of the alpacas and llamas. The vicuñas were so profoundly valued among the Inca that the fleece was saved for Incan eminence.

4.   Chile

Chile is unlike any other country I have visited in South America. Because of its natural beauty, high literacy rate, and fairly stable political situation, it can be best described as the Switzerland of the south. Chile is a paradise for nature lovers and outdoor enthusiasts. Within the country, one can find a diverse variety of landscapes including vineyards, volcanoes, deserts, beaches, lakes, glaciers and forests. Nature, culture, food and people just are few of the reasons to visit Chile.

1. Easter Island, Chile

One of Chile's primary normal vacation spots, the Atacama Desert is an interesting climate to observe. Encircled by dazzling view, the Atacama desert offers a fountain of liquid magma dabbed skyline and a practically outsider scene. You will likewise appreciate probably the best put on Earth for stargazing. To visit the desert, you can show up at the entryway town of San Pedro. Indeed, even San Pedro merits investigating as there are diverse alluring roads, squares, and structures.

The outsider scene is helped along by the way that this is the world's driest desert for certain territories always failing to have encountered downpour in written history. Since the zone is so dry, there is next to no vegetation. A large portion of the desert is totally missing vegetation. You can walk a huge number of miles without experiencing any indication of life.

2. The Atacama Desert, Chile

One of Chile's primary normal vacation spots, the Atacama Desert is an interesting climate to observe. Encircled by dazzling view, the Atacama desert offers a fountain of liquid magma dabbed skyline and a practically outsider scene. You will likewise appreciate probably the best put on Earth for stargazing. To visit the desert, you can show up at the entryway town of San Pedro. Indeed, even San Pedro merits investigating as there are diverse alluring roads, squares, and structures. The outsider scene is helped along by the way that this is the world's driest desert for certain territories always failing to have encountered downpour in written history.

Since the zone is so dry, there is next to no vegetation. A large portion of the desert is totally missing vegetation. You can walk a huge number of miles without experiencing any indication of life. Not simply an attract to sightseers keen on visiting the zone, the Atacama Desert is likewise a draw for NASA. The Atacama doesn't just seem as though an outsider scene, yet soil tests uncover a comparable soil to zones on Mars. Along these lines, NASA utilizes the territory as a proving ground for investigation and for recording TV narratives about different universes. The Atacama additionally contains proof of human home from near 10,000 years prior. Proof of vegetation has likewise been found from millennia prior clarifying how individuals settled here. During this time, it's idea the desert was marshland lavish with vegetation.

3. The Termas Geométricas, Chile

Situated in Chile's Lake Locale in a territory called Pucon, you will locate some awesome warm spas. A most loved is called Termas Geométricas with its Japanese motivated plan with spans twisting past the pools, cascades, and backwoods. In the region, you can discover 17 underground aquifers which lay in a gully covered with rich green vegetation. Specked around the territory are the pools and cascades, which you can discover utilizing the unpredictably planned footpath.

Albeit the walkway has been intended to bring to the table a differentiation to the normal background, the man made designs actually mix with the scene. For instance, albeit the changing room hovels are made with similar red wood as the pathways, they have been planted with vegetation on the rooftop expanding the common background.

4.   Huaraz & the Huascarán National Park, Peru

Quite possibly the most visited and appealing pieces of the Andes mountain range, the Huascarán Public Park ensures a zone of the Andes known as the Cordillera Blanca. Inside and encompassing the recreation center, you can locate some lovely glacial masses and tidal ponds.

Regardless of whether you're not intrigued by concentrated climbs or hiking, a portion of these can be visited on day climbs from the door city of Huaraz. The territory secures Mount Huascaran, which is Peru's biggest mountain and gives the public park its name. There are various creatures and plants to see around the recreation center, including the renowned vicuñas. These are the antiquated precursors of the alpacas and llamas. The vicuñas were so profoundly valued among the Inca that the fleece was saved for Incan eminence.

5. Ecuador

Although Ecuador may be small, it's a destination that's got it all! This diverse country that boasts a rich cultural heritage, fine food, the Amazon jungle and Andean highlands is SO worth exploring for itself! Whether you're planning a trip the Galapagos or are looking for a rewarding destination on its own, read on to find out why you should visit Ecuador and what to do once you get there. **From tropical beaches to stunning landscapes, indigenous markets and historical towns, Ecuador is often suggested as the ideal destination for anyone wanting a taste of the best of South America.**

1. The Galapagos Islands, Ecuador

The Galapagos Islands are a natural life rich heaven off the bank of Ecuador. Appreciate wonderful sea shores, unspoiled tropical coves, phenomenal view, and a portion of the world's most unbelievable natural life encounters. The archipelago is world popular as assisting Charles Darwin with finding how the world's untamed life turned out to be so assorted, as it assisted him with understanding development by normal choice.

Since the Galapagos Islands were one of the last world regions to be found, joined with having not many hunters, the creatures are cordial and inquisitive. Appreciate recognizing all the notable types of the Galapagos Islands, including monster turtles, marine iguanas, blue-footed boobies, frigatebirds, ocean lions, pelicans, and Darwin's finches.

2. Ecuador's Cloud Forest

The cloud backwoods are woodland characterized at a particularly high elevation that it is among the mists. In South America, the cloud backwoods are along the slants of the Andes and is one of the world's most extravagant regions for creature and vegetation. Appreciate guided visits through the cloud backwoods to locate some phenomenal creatures and plants. This is a particularly incredible territory to see excellent orchids and bromeliads sticking to the trees.

Among the rich vegetation, you can likewise discover a wide range of creatures. The cloud timberland is especially plentiful with ummingbirds and there are over a hundred distinct animal groups to discover. There are additionally some bigger creatures living in the cloud timberland. You can risk upon wooly monkeys, capuchins, and even spectacled bears albeit these are once in a while seen. Ecuador is a phenomenal spot to appreciate the cloud woods and an enthusiastically suggested hold up is called Mashpi Cabin, which offers rich stays and guided visits with a naturally cognizant way to deal with the travel industry.

3. The Machalilla National Park, Ecuador

On the Ecuadorian coast, you can locate the fabulous Machalilla Public Park. The recreation center secures the woods of South America's Pacific Coast, which keeps on being one of the world's most compromised living spaces. Machalilla Public Park secures just shy of 100,000 sections of land (40,000 hectares) of dry tropical timberland, seaward islands, a significant length of the seashore, and 50,000 sections of land (20,000 hectares) of beachfront waters.

The recreation center secures a wide range of creatures and plants. Living in the backwoods are various monkeys, brocket deer, vivid toxic substance dart frogs, sloths, peccary, panther, and a wide range of winged animals and brilliant butterflies. The beachfront waters are then home to humpback whales, ocean turtles, manta beams, and a high variety of fish. This is additionally an extraordinary spot to take off on a whale watching visits as humpbacks make their yearly relocation to the recreation center from June to October. Notwithstanding lovely landscape and natural life, the recreation center contains some significant archeological destinations.

4. Banos, Ecuador

A mainstream territory of Ecuador, Banos is known for the various natural aquifers, excellent landscape, and experience exercises. This is quite possibly the most famous traveler objections in Ecuador and is frequently visited in mix with the Galapagos and the Amazon Rainforest.

In any case, the primary draws are the staggering landscape and the phenomenal warm springs the locale was named after. The landscape is lavish and offers some awesome perspectives. You can discover more than 60 distinct cascades and some can be watched while appreciating the natural aquifers themselves. The biggest and most acclaimed cascade in the area is called Pailón del Diablo, which was named after the state of the pool underneath.

6. Bolivia

Celebrated for its colorful history, fascinating customs, diverse wildlife and jaw-dropping landscapes, Bolivia is a country like no other. The heart of South America empowers travelers to expand their horizons, paving the way for unique encounters at every twist and turn. While it's true that much of Bolivia isn't set up for tourism, those willing to take the path less traveled are rewarded with eye-opening experiences, adventurous activities, and stunning photo opportunities, not to mention epic stories to tell the folks back home.

1. Salar De Uyuni, Bolivia

In the event that you have seen the photographs playing with point of view on salt pads, odds are these were taking at the Salar De Uyuni in Bolivia. Albeit the photographs are on numerous individuals' brains when visiting the salt pads, the actual district is likewise captivating to see. As the world's biggest salt level, the Salar De Uyuni covers an amazing territory of a little more than 4,000 square miles (10,300 km²). Seeing this unfathomable scene merits the visit and watching the dawn and nightfall here is particularly charming.

The salt is really an outside on an enormous lake, which makes an outsider and barren scene. Seeing the salt pads of a day is a totally extraordinary, yet similarly tremendous, experience from seeing it around evening time. Albeit apparently uninhabited, there are a few creatures and plants that live here. You can see some various prickly plants and even flamingos visit over the wetter months.

2. Salar de Uyuni

Salar de Uyuni is the greatest salt level on the planet. Perhaps the most well-known attractions in Salar de Uyuni is a graveyard for trains! It contains all the trains that were utilized in mining during the 1940s and presently draws in a large number of sightseers consistently.

3. Uyuni's National Parks

Explorers travel to the public parks encompassing the Southern desert town of Uyuni for the sights of the salt pads alone. Be that as it may, if you book a three-day (or more) visit from Uyuni, you'll be reimbursed with a lot more mind-boggling sees on top of the epic salt pads. Prepare to see volcanoes, mountains, and vast territories of the desert, and set yourself up for a scope of environments as you drive more than 11,995 feet above ocean level.

On the off chance that you have your brains about you (and a consistent hand), you can swim through the marshes around a portion of the area's lakes to catch a photograph of the flamingos who settle there to rest and take care of. It's well worth expanding your visit through the salt pads to remember a more significant amount of Bolivia's best everyday marvels. Try not to pass up a great opportunity!

7. Colombia

Colombia is an amazing country, bursting with vibrant cities, unmissable tourist attractions and hundreds of things to do. Here we act as your guide and answer your top ten travel and tourism questions. Colombia is one of the world's most diverse countries with two oceans, a range of climates, energetic cities, astonishing wildlife and things to do including kayaking, rafting, rock climbing, paragliding, surfing, diving, dancing and more.

e

1. Cartagena, Colombia

One of Colombia's most lovely urban areas, Cartagena offers some generally entrancing and bright roads. Appreciate the sentimental rear entryways and complicatedly planned houses of prayer in the UNESCO perceived Old Town. While strolling around Old Town, you can appreciate some intricate squares with wellsprings, alluring wooden galleries, and see the noteworthy manors of the Spanish pilgrims. The city outside of the memorable focus is additionally an awesome spot to appreciate.

From Old Town, the city reaches out into an advanced South American city with numerous phenomenal eateries, bistros, exhibition halls, and activities. As Cartagena is situated on Colombia's Caribbean Coast, the city is a standard port of call for some, Caribbean travels.

2. The Parque Tayrona, Colombia

This is apparently Colombia's best-secured territory. The recreation center is found simply under an hour's drive from St Nick Marta or four hours from Cartagena on the Caribbean Coast. The excellence of the region is that the rainforest squeezes straight facing the wonderful palm-tree bordered seashore. You can appreciate spotting various feathered creatures and even monkeys in and around the recreation center. The monkeys you can find in the recreation center incorporate howler monkeys, capuchins, and tamarins. The brilliant sands and trees give a picture of heaven and it's an awesome spot to unwind.

The scene is additionally delightful with the Sierra Nevada de St Nick Marta mountain range out of sight. There are likewise various paths to appreciate through the recreation center. Notwithstanding the untamed life and excellent view.

3. Medellin, Colombia

As one of Colombia's favorite cities for visitors, Medellin has become a top tourist destination. Enjoy a friendly and lively city with many fascinating sights and things to do.

Medellin offers a very pleasant year round temperature, many restaurants serving delicious cuisine, and vibrant nightlife.

Around Medellin, you can enjoy boutique cafes, great bars, many city parks, and great shopping opportunities. There are also various interesting museums, a butterfly house, and the botanical gardens to explore.

Salsa dancing is also a favorite things to try in Medellin and there are numerous salsa schools to teach you the basics. You can then head out at night to one of the many latin clubs.

This is also a good place to learn Spanish, which will help you in your travels around Colombia and to other South American countries. There are many different Spanish schools to choose from.

4. The Zona Cafetera, Colombia

For coffee darlings, the Zona Cafetera offers an opportunity to see where your coffee is developed. Colombia is a primary exporter of coffee and the Zona Cafetera gives the ideal spot to get familiar with the beverage. You can appreciate visiting the coffee ranches while examining numerous cups of new Arabica coffee along the way.

There are numerous bistros all through the district to appreciate a portion of the world's freshest coffee. While at the homesteads, you can see the coffee beans filling in the fields. You would then be able to appreciate a visit that takes you through the cycle of how this winds up in your #1 coffee cup.

8. Guyana

The South American continent, with its relics of ancient civilizations, millions of square kilometers of dense jungle that pumps oxygen out into the world and rich cultures that have survived invasions and epidemics, has become far more accessible to global travelers. Kaieteur Falls in Guyana, South America and a hidden secret. Guyana is South America's best-kept secret. But I guarantee that for every country you might have visited, there are number you've never heard of. Despite its profusion of pristine rainforest, larger-than-life wildlife and cultural heritage with roots across the globe, Guyana is one of those.

1. The Kaieteur Falls, Guyana

Another amazing waterfall, Kaieteur Falls is a lesser known fascination in the little nation of Guyana on the Guiana Shield of northeastern South America. The Kaieteur Falls is one of the world's most noteworthy single drop waterfalls at 820 feet (250 m). Despite the fact that Heavenly messenger Falls is significantly taller, Kaieteur Falls has a course with substantially more water and can be 400 feet (122 m) wide over the wetter months. The waterfall sits in the phenomenal Kaieteur Public Park.

As one of the most seasoned in South America, this park is home to some phenomenal untamed life. Indeed, even close to the falls there's an opportunity to see the energetically shaded Guianan chicken of-the-rock with its wonderful red plumage. Different creatures to discover incorporate brilliant frogs, peccary, otters, brocket deer, and various monkeys

2. Kaieteur National Park

The Potaro-Siparuni district's gem is a huge and extensive secured zone that ascents and falls with the incredible defense edges of the Guyana tepuis. Wearing thick, monkey-specked, panther followed rainforests and covering an incredible 62,000 hectares, it's hailed as the country's ecotourist focal point.

And keeping in mind that the biodiversity and immaculate virgin woods are genuine pulls, the masterpiece here is irrefutably the Kaieteur Falls.

Falling an astonishing 226 meters down the ledges of the Pacaraima Mountains, this smaller person, both the Niagara and Victoria Falls, the same and cast a crest of the tropical fog into the wilderness air in general.

3. Mount Roraima

Arguably the most glorious of all the South American tepuis, sheer-cut Mount Roraima is a tabletop mountain that rises like a petrified oblong of chiseled rock, right on the edge of Venezuela, Brazil and Guyana.Largely unknown, the mountain is actually one of the most ancient geological formations on the planet, with its roots back in the Precambrian period more than two billion years ago.

It lurches vertically from the ground, soaring 400-meters straight up from the grasslands and woods below.

A challenge even for the most experienced hikers and mountain climbers, the top of the plateau here is a treasure box of natural wonders, with uber-rare pitcher plants and algae, reptilians and amphibians inhabiting the summit, untouched and unhindered by the predators in the flats below.

9. Venezuela

Venezuela, home to some of South America's most incredible landscapes, rightly has a terrible image problem at the moment. Hyperinflation has led to a dramatic drop in living standards and issues with the supply of basic goods, while personal safety, particularly in Caracas, is worse than anywhere else on the continent. Thousands of its own citizens have fled the country and spread throughout South America (it's estimated more than two million have left since 2014). While visiting can be incredibly cheap because of the black-market value of the dollar/euro, safety is a serious concern.

Few countries in the world have this degree of natural beauty: Andean peaks, Caribbean coastline, idyllic islands, grasslands teeming with wildlife, the steamy Orinoco Delta.

1. Angel Falls, Venezuela

As the world's biggest single drop waterfall, Angel Falls is one of the world's most well-known waterfalls and sits in a separated zone a short departure from Ciudad Bolívar. Falling down Mount Auyantepui, Angel Falls is Venezuela's most famous vacation destination and is around multiple times taller than Nevada Falls in the USA at 807 meters (2,648 feet). Broadly, the falls is named after Jimmy Angel after he slammed his plane on top of Auyantepui in 1937.

You will arrive at the falls from the close by town of Canaima. From here, you will appreciate a boat trip down the Carrao Stream through the backwoods prior to arriving at the falls. The actual falls are situated inside the Canaima Public Park, which is likewise a fabulous region to visit. The recreation center covers 12,000 square miles (30,000 km2) of backwoods and savanna dabbed with emotional tabletop mountains.

2. Isla de Margarita

Isla de Margarita is considered in evolved sea shore places in Venezuela. Lying roughly 40 kilometers north of the terrain, this is one of Venezuela's significant vacationer locations for sun searchers. The island's primary attractions are the lovely delicate sand seashores, famous for the two outsiders and Venezuelans.

Many sanction flights fly straightforwardly to Isla Margarita from an assortment of global objections. Still, at the same time, it's conceivable to take a ship to the island from Puerto La Cruz on the territory.

The island's fundamental city is Porlamar, yet the various seashores are spread around the island, probably the best on the north and east sides. A large number of these are created, with lodgings or cafés. The absolute most well-known seashores are La Playa El Agua, Playa Puerto Cruz, Playa Guacuco, and Playa Manzanillo.

3. Canaima National Park

Canaima National Park covers 3,000,000 hectares and is recorded as an UNESCO World Heritage Site. It is generally connected with Angel Falls and the region around Canaima, however this is in reality just a little region of the unfathomably different park.

The recreation center likewise envelops La Gran Sabana's high level and incorporates more than 100 tepuis (table-top mountains), which rise in excess of 1,000 meters over the savannahs. An outing through the Gran Sabana and Canaima National Park is a novel encounter. It doesn't really should be joined with an excursion to Angel Falls, especially during the dry season.

Features around there are the various cascades spread across the whole locale, especially in the Gran Sabana close to the Brazilian line. Swimming at the base of the cascades is one of the features and can give an invigorating break from the noontime sun's warmth during the dry season.

CONCLUSION

Life is full of so many opportunities and adventures, while it depends on the person who is willing to take risk and do so much in life, if you do not take stance right now how you will know the unparalleled beauty around the world, or wander what you have missed in life. Life gives do much chances and it is on us how we take them granted for ourselves. world is full of places and sites which we cannot even imagine in life but are worth seeing and now I have given you the opportunity to see the glimpse of world here and now up to you now, how you enjoy yourselves in 2021 after so much troubles and tragedies.

CPSIA information can be obtained
at www.ICGtesting.com
Printed in the USA
BVHW051332020321
601493BV00015B/1283